Freedom Mantra

Kumar Anu

Invincible Publishers

First Printing: 2020

ISBN: 978-93-89600-24-7

Registered Address: 201A, SAS Tower, Sector 38, Gurgaon - 122003

For Krishna

Table of Contents

Prologue

This is the story of Freedom.

Freedom from the guilt, fear, and anger that resides in most of us. Freedom from the bondage of limitless desires that control our life. This is the story of a single mantra, a single philosophy, and a single practice that liberates us from suffering.

A few years ago, at an international airport, I met a self-made Billionaire Monk who transformed my life. That day at the airport, he revealed the secret of his success and answered some of my toughest questions. He became my Guru, my Guide, and my Teacher. He spoke about Freedom, about Work, and about Life.

In this book, I share his wisdom.

* * *

At a very young age, I discovered that I was a restless soul. For a good part of my life, I was in search of something. However, I could never define that something. I searched for a supernatural power that could change my destiny, bring prosperity, and grant permanent happiness.

I traveled the world to find God, happiness, peace, wealth, fame, and—you guessed it—everything.

And in the midst of this search, I found freedom. And this is the story of my transformation from a restless soul to a liberated soul. This story is not about secret rituals, it's not about magical powers, and it's not about religious practices. This story is based on my experiences with life, the people I have met, and the scriptures I have read.

Before liberation, as far as my memory goes, I could not spend a single minute with myself. If I had free time, I had to do something. I lived in an autopilot mode and worked hard to secure my future, always planning for the next move.

My addiction to excessive thinking was beyond control. Thinking never stopped—while I was eating, while I was driving, while I was talking, and even while I was sleeping. For many consecutive days, I got up in the morning, exhausted and tired—as if I'd been watching a movie the entire night in my dreams.

Thoughts of work, fantasies of becoming rich, daydreams of making good friends, anything, and everything—the constant stream of thoughts never stopped.

Often, I found myself walking on the streets, talking to myself for hours. Yes, I could talk to myself for hours.

Occasionally, to my surprise, I found myself in a state of boredom, as if there was nothing to do, nothing that could excite me, and nothing that could bring happiness.

I picked up regular arguments with my friends and family. My resentment, my anger, and my intolerance for others were out of control. I became an expert in the blame game. Words like forgiveness and compassion were not in my dictionary.

In a nutshell, I was a wild animal making bad choices. The animal was greedy, restless, and selfish. Motivated by limitless desire, I was ready to do anything to satisfy my thirst.

Watching television, reading novels, surfing internet, eating food, and partying with restless souls—I looked all over the place to find happiness. My search for this 'unknown something' made me so anxious that I started consuming alcohol every day. I thought alcohol would solve my problems. And as expected, it did not.

My search continued—I had to find another path.

I met a group of fellow seekers who suggested that fasting could give me the power to make my dreams come true. Hence, I began to fast regularly. I did that for some time, often eating just one meal a day. After a few months, I realized that I was fighting with my body and losing my energy. Eventually, I gave up.

My search continued—I had to find another path.

I started listening to sages, saints, priests, and pastors. I started wearing lucky charms and amulets to change my life. Nothing worked.

My search continued—I had to find another path.

And then, as done by many others, I took seven dips into the holy rivers to wash away my bad Karma.

I studied and practiced many religions but could never connect with any God of any religion.

My search continued—I had to find another path.

I was in search of answers. Why am I so restless? What is happiness? How do I become rich and successful? There had to be a secret path that could bring me complete freedom. All my questions boiled down to a simple question:

What is the path to freedom?

This book will show you that path. It's a tough path—but—freedom is assured.

The Free Soul

A few years later, at an international airport, I saw an old man walking slowly toward the check-in counter. That day the weather was terrible—cloudy, rainy, and poor visibility. Most of the flights were delayed, and people were losing their patience. However, this human being was very calm, serene, and was smiling at everyone.

In the crowded airport, he seemed to be the only person who was simply at the airport. Others were someplace else—playing on their mobile phones, updating their social media statuses, watching world news, or like me, planning continuously about their futures.

After completing check-in, this person sat on a chair close to his boarding gate, which was adjacent to my boarding gate. So, I just stood there and started watching him.

The aura of this old man was radiating all over. Though I wanted to talk to him, I was very hesitant, so I walked towards him and sat on the vacant chair next to him.

He looked at me and smiled. He had this peaceful energy around him that made me feel so comfortable. I was not thinking anymore; I was just there.

At that moment, I gathered some courage to speak to him.

"How do you radiate so much peaceful energy around you? I mean, what do you do that makes you so happy? Who are you?" I asked.

"I am a Free Soul."

He replied.

"What do Free Souls do?" I questioned with curiosity.

"Free Souls practice freedom, through a simple mantra, that liberates them from the bondage of Karma."

He replied.

I did not like that answer. And I surely wanted to give it back. Over the years, I had met people who look for an opportunity to advise, who look for an opportunity to promote their religion, and who look for an opportunity to convert seekers into their sect.

"Not to offend you, but I believe you belong to some religious sect. And people of your tribe are escapists. They run away from reality, they run away from their desires, and they run away from their own lives.

It is very easy to sit under a tree to meditate with a mantra and do nothing in the real world."

I said, and I tried to suppress my anger that was surfacing from my past experiences.

"Real life is hard work. It's filled with hundreds of emotions, and it's very painful at times."

I added.

I was sarcastic, rude, and burning with anger.

He smiled.

"What makes you think that Free Souls sit under the tree and meditate. In order to convince you, let me tell you that I run my own business of software development. And my business is valued around one billion US dollars. I am a hard-working soul. And I am free from any bondage."

He said.

I have to admit, at that moment, that I was speechless. I was quiet for a few seconds, but then he smiled again, and looked deeply into my eyes.

"You don't believe me?" He questioned, handing over his business card to me.

At this moment, I realized that there were few other people in corporate suits sitting behind him. Also, a well-built person was sitting next to him, who looked like his bodyguard.

As I looked over the business card that revealed his identity, I became speechless. And as my mind tried to compose itself, I even thought of taking a selfie with him. But I was too embarrassed to talk anymore.

He smiled and said, "There is nothing wrong in having a big house, a big car, or a big business. The human suffering starts when we get attached to them."

"Who are you, my dear friend?" He asked.

"I am a writer." I replied.

"That is what you do," he said. "I would like to know who you are."

And again, he looked deeply into my eyes. Maybe he saw the struggle inside me.

"Let me ask you a different question," he laughed and said, "What are you seeking? What is your story?"

I paused for a few moments as I looked at him. I felt hesitant and comfortable at the same time—hesitant because I was talking to a stranger and comfortable because of the positive aura around him. After a few moments of reflection, I decided to share my life and my struggle.

I told him about my restlessness, about my messed-up relationships, about my visits to the temples and the shrines, about my drive for success and fame, and about my search to find freedom.

He was listening, deeply listening. He gave his hundred percent to me.

After about ten minutes of talking, I was done. I had nothing more to say. For the first time in my life, someone had listened to me without interrupting me, without making judgments about me, and without dividing their attention.

He smiled at me again and started talking.

"Eighty years on planet Earth, I have learned one thing, that all problems disappear on their own. In fact, the problems turn into something beautiful. The problems are here to teach us something. "

He Said.

"Have you heard about Karma?"

He asked.

"Yes. You reap what you sow. If you do good, you will receive good; if you do bad, you will receive bad. Good Karma is heaven; Bad Karma is hell. I think all the religions of the world agree on just this one concept."

I replied.

He smiled again.

"If I told you that there is a method to change the cycle of Karma in your favor and find everlasting freedom, will you practice that method?" He asked.

"Of course, I would."

I replied.

"But I don't think we can find freedom."

I added. And, I was restless again.

"Yes, we can. And we do this by following a simple mantra practiced by Free Souls for over five thousand years."

He said.

"We call it the Freedom Mantra."

He added.

"And, what is the Mantra?"

I asked.

"I do my duties free from rewards."

He replied.

He looked into my eyes, still smiling at me. I, however, gave him a hopeless look.

"I gave you the secret of my freedom. Try to comprehend it."

He added.

"I do my duties free from rewards."

He said again.

"How can this mantra change the cycle of Karma to embrace freedom?" I asked.

"Listen, my friend, when we are not attached or repelled by the rewards of our action—we free ourselves from the bondage of Karma.

I do my duties, not because I have the desire for rewards, not because of profit-loss, and not because of success-failure. I do my duties because they are propelled by my inborn nature, and they have to be done.

It is the desire of the reward that creates bondage and suffering. The actions performed to accomplish our duties are free from suffering. If you focus on the act and not on the results, you free yourself from the bondage of desire.

And when you free yourself from the bondage of desire, you change the cycle of Karma, and you find Freedom."

He replied.

"How can you assure me that I will find freedom through this practice?" I asked.

"The beauty of Freedom Mantra is that its practice brings immediate peace, immediate joy, and immediate freedom.

This is not a blind faith, that works sometimes and fails sometimes. The Freedom Mantra is a logical practice that delivers instantaneously.

Practice the mantra for an hour, and you will be peaceful for that hour. Practice the mantra for a day, in every activity that you undertake, and you will be satisfied and contented throughout the day.

The practice of Freedom Mantra is not a belief-based system. It is a proof-based system. And it delivers freedom, instantaneously."

He replied.

"How can I get Freedom instantaneously?" I asked.

"We find Freedom immediately because we derive joy from work and not from its rewards. There is a big difference in working for your duties and working for your rewards. When you work for your duties, you work for work's sake; you are enjoying the work.

And with Freedom Mantra, when you work on a task, you give your complete dedication to it. When you are free from rewards, you are free from the success or failure of that task. In this way, you are not postponing your joy; you experience joy in the present moment.

However, if you are stuck on rewards, you postpone your joy to a future date because the outcome is delivered in the future. The Freedom Mantra teaches us not to postpone our joy, but to enjoy life right here right now."

He replied.

The Freedom Mantra

"I do my duties free from rewards."

He repeated the Freedom Mantra.

He got me engaged in a conversation. I wanted to know more about his secret. And I started asking countless questions about the mantra. He replied to my questions with calmness and clarity.

"What is a mantra?" I asked.

"A mantra is a meaningful thought, a set of words, that are repeated frequently in the mind.

The word mantra is a combination of two words, 'Mann' which translates to the mind, and 'Tra' which translates to a vehicle.

Mantra is a vehicle of the mind. And Freedom Mantra is that special vehicle, which takes you towards freedom as soon as you start it."

He replied.

"The more I work, the more I get entangled into bondage. Why does the Freedom Mantra talk about doing?" I asked.

"Free Souls embrace freedom through work. But not the way the majority of humanity works. Humans work to seek rewards. Free Souls work but are free from rewards. They are not concerned about winning or losing; they are only concerned about working. This approach eliminates bondage.

Work is Worship for the Free Soul, and we don't miss a beat on doing our work. The part **'I do'** in the freedom Mantra is an essential component in the practice. Doing is the key. Laziness is evil for the Free Soul.

Hence if you wish to embrace freedom, you have to destroy laziness, you have to find every opportunity to work, and you have to dedicate yourself to your duties."

He replied.

"What are Duties?" I asked.

"The Freedom Mantra speaks about **'my duties'**. And there is a deep meaning hidden in the word **'my'**. Each person has a specific set of duties, and their duties should not be influenced by what others are doing.

Duties are the tasks and activities that we need to do to accomplish the purpose of our life. For e.g. taking care of our family, doing our daily job, cultivating our talents, doing our daily chores. These are all our duties. In general, duties are of two types:

Obligatory Duties:

Our obligatory duties are duties that align with the stage of our life. These are the duties that have to be done, even if you don't like them. Every person goes through multiple stages in life. These stages are broadly classified into four categories—childhood, young adult, middle age, and retired life. Each stage has a different set of obligatory duties.

Sometimes, we do not want to do our obligatory duties because we find then boring, tiresome, and thankless. For example, cleaning our house, or working at a job that is not gratifying. However, we should utilize these obligatory duties as a means to practice the Freedom Mantra. Because, when we keep doing these duties with complete dedication and free from rewards, we find peace and fulfillment.

Inborn Duties:

Inborn Duties are duties that help us express our inner being. Every person is born with a set of strengths, and every person inclines towards a specific area of work. These two aspects build our nature and help us identify our Inborn Duties. This set of duties could be our daily job, or this could be our hobby, or this could be our passion.

The inborn duties can never harm us because they are born along with us. They reflect our true nature."

He replied.

"Can you explain duties, sorry, as you mentioned, "my duties," with an example?" I asked.

"Let me explain "my duties" with poison and nectar.

A poisonous worm is born on the web of poison. This poison is life to the worm. It's the duty of the worm, that propels it, to produce poison.

A honey bee, on the other hand, feeds itself from the nectar of flowers. This nectar is life to the honey bee. It's the duty of the honey bee, that propels it, to produce honey.

However, if this poisonous worm comes in contact with honey, it will die immediately. Similarly, if the honey bee comes in contact with poison, it will die instantly. What is death for the honey bee, is life for the worm. And what is death for the worm, is life for the honey bee. This is how nature is created.

Similarly, as humans, we also have our obligatory duties and inborn duties. We should do our duties and not get influenced by what others are doing. If we do what we are supposed to do, we do not obstruct the flow of life. "

He replied.

"What are Rewards?" Was my next question.

"To understand rewards, you have to understand attachments-repulsions. Because attachments-repulsions are the root thought behind rewards.

Rewards are created by our attachments-repulsions to the objects (People, Things, Situations) in the outer world. Attachments-repulsions are dualities of life that get transformed into good rewards or bad rewards. Attachment is seeking a good reward. Repulsion is de-seeking a bad reward.

Attachment is clinging to a likeable object (People, Things, Situations) in the outer world. Once there is attachment to the object, the mind will keep bringing thoughts of that object. Eventually, when attachment gains energy, the mind will declare that there is no happiness without that object.

Repulsion is clinging to an unlikable object (People, Things, Situations) in the outer world. Once there is repulsion to the object, the mind will keep bringing thoughts of that object. Eventually, when repulsion gains energy, the mind will declare that there is no happiness until you destroy that object.

Attachments-repulsions, for rewards, are unwanted software programs running in the hardware of the mind. Attachments-Repulsions, for rewards, are not the objects of the outer world. They are mental energies around those objects in the inner world.

Attachments-repulsions, for rewards, cloud the mind, and destroy the power of discrimination. People, things, and situations don't appear as they are. This destroys the human capability to make better decisions.

Human beings are inside a cage that isolates them from freedom. Attachment is a golden cage. Repulsion is an iron cage. Both of these cages are the cause of human suffering. Free Souls let go of the golden cage. Free Souls let go of the iron cage. And then, they embrace freedom.

Once you understand the true meaning of Attachments-Repulsions, it will become very easy for you to do your work free from rewards.

Attachment = Success = Good Reward.

Repulsion = Failure = Bad Reward.

Attachment = Pleasing Situation = Good Reward.
Repulsion=Unpleasing Situation = Bad Reward.

Attachment = Saved Wealth = Good Reward.
Repulsion = Loss of Wealth = Bad Reward.

Attachment = Friends = Good Reward.
Repulsion = Enemies = Bad Reward.

Attachment = Pleasant Emotions = Good Reward.
Repulsion = Painful Emotions = Bad Reward.

Attachment = Excitement = Good Reward.
Repulsion = Boredom = Bad Reward.

Attachment = Happiness = Good Reward.
Repulsion = Unhappiness = Bad Reward.

The mind has a tendency to stick to both good rewards and bad rewards. It has a tendency to seek attachments and repulsions. And the Freedom Mantra breaks this tendency."

He replied.

"I understand that the mind wants to stick to attachments or good rewards. But why would the mind stick to repulsions or bad rewards?" I asked.

"The mind does not distinguish between attachments and repulsions. For the mind, they are the same juice in different containers.

The mind sees the favorable and the unfavorable through the same lens. It wants to stick to both good rewards and bad rewards.

The objects we like—generate the same energy—as the objects we dislike."

He replied.

"Can you elaborate on the idea of being Free from Rewards?" I asked.

"The phrase **'Free from Rewards'** has a profound meaning. It is the essence of the Freedom Mantra. It is the idea that helps us find liberation through our work.

When we are free from rewards, the attachments-repulsions fizzle out—and on the other side—when we let go attachments-repulsions, we become free from rewards.

Free from rewards can be explained in two parts :

Free from Rewards = The art of letting go of the energy of attachments-repulsions for rewards.

To be free from the energy of attachments-repulsions involves acknowledging this energy and then dropping this energy. This is a mental act, and there is a method to do this. (Discussed in the chapter, Understanding the Mind)

Free from Rewards = The art of being balanced with the dualities of life.

To be balanced with the dualities of life is to treat alike success-failure, happiness-sorrow, good-evil, excitement-boredom, and so on. This equanimity is achieved through understanding and will power. (Discussed throughout the book)

With this insight, the Freedom Mantra can be loosely translated into the following:

I do my duties free from rewards.

I do my duties free from good rewards or bad rewards.

I do my duties free from attachments or repulsions.

I do my duties free from likes and dislikes.

I do my duties free from happiness or sorrow.

I do my duties free from success or failure.

I do my duties free from pain or pleasure.

I do my duties free from pleasant or unpleasant.

When we are free from rewards, we are reprograming the mind to stop seeking the objects of our attachments-repulsions and to treat alike happiness and sorrow."

He replied.

"What is the point of all this, if I do not enjoy my rewards and disown them?" I asked.

"I am not suggesting that you do not enjoy your rewards and disown them. I am suggesting that your work should be free from rewards.

After your practice becomes steady, you will reach a state of freedom. In this state, you will be okay if you get your rewards, and you will be okay if you don't get your rewards.

Enjoying your rewards and being free from your rewards are two different things."

He replied.

"Attachment to good rewards and repulsion to bad rewards, keep me grounded. Why should I not

seek them?" I asked.

"Attachments-repulsions to rewards, good or bad, are the prime cause of suffering in the world. Attachments-repulsions lead to greed, frustration, and wrong actions.

When the object of attachment-repulsion is fulfilled, we develop greed. When the object of attachment-repulsion is unfulfilled, we develop frustration. And both greed and frustration lead to wrong actions.

It's your illusion that makes you think that rewards keep you grounded. The truth is that there is only one thing that keeps human beings grounded—and that is freedom.

The purpose of human life is to find freedom because freedom brings joy—never ending joy. "

He replied.

"How can I do my duties free from rewards? This thought is very contradictory. Can you explain?" I asked.

"We only have control only on our work, not on the rewards. Many factors deliver a reward—Divine will, actions of other people involved, the timing of your actions, and your previous Karmas.

And beyond that, the rewards are for the Divine to move the world forward. We are doing a service to the Divine through our duties.

And the definition of Divine depends on your belief system. Divine can be Universe, Collective Consciousness, or God."

He replied.

"What is the uniqueness of the Freedom Mantra?

"I asked.

"This practice enables the Free Soul to focus on a single idea, a single resolute, and a single goal.

In today's world, there is an overload of information. If you read a life transformative book, it will talk about ten laws, seven rules, five habits, three mindsets, and so on. However, the Freedom Mantra is just one idea that transforms life.

Any other practice will require you to do too many things, and that will make your intellect multi branched. And with a multi branched intellect, you will reach now where.

But with Freedom Mantra, the intellect decides to focus on just one idea. With this single pointed intellect, when you keep your focus on the Freedom Mantra, and when you keep practicing the mantra, again and again—Freedom is assured.

Also, with a single practice, the Freedom Mantra takes care of our inner world and the outer world. It brings peace of mind in the inner world because we are free from rewards. And it brings satisfaction of work in the outer world because we are focused on our work and defocused from the outcome."

He replied.

"**Is there any religious reference to the Freedom Mantra?** "I asked.

"All the religions of the world talk about the Freedom Mantra, but their context is different.

Christianity teaches, 'Be in this world, but not of this world.'

Hinduism teaches, 'Focusing on your actions and not on the fruits of your actions.'

Buddhism teaches,' The root of all suffering is attachment.'

Islam teaches, 'Don't be attached, by greed, for more and more.'

It is the same message presented in a different way. "

He replied.

"Can you give me an example from your own life?" I asked.

"I started practicing the Freedom Mantra when my son was born. In fact, his birth helped me understand the mantra.

My son was born with a severe case of Autism. Right after his birth, we understood that he would struggle through life, and he will need fulltime assistance.

Initially, I was very disappointed. My first reaction was—why did this happen to me? What wrong have I done? How am I going to survive? I lost hope in life and cried and cried for many days.

And then amid this suffering, I found the Freedom Mantra. As I started practicing the mantra and when my practice became strong—I understood that Autism was something that happened to my son, and nothing happened to me. I realized that my duty as a parent was to make sure that he gets all the love and support he needs.

I separated myself from my suffering and focused on my duties. Freedom Mantra transformed my life."

He replied.

"What happens when we find freedom?" I asked.

"Freedom purifies the mind and brings permanent Joy.

Joy and Happiness are two separate states. Happiness depends on an external object, and joy is a reflection of our inner Self.

Joy is born the moment we are free from attachments-repulsions and the moment we treat alike pain or pleasure; boredom or excitement; happiness or suffering."

He replied.

"Why do you call this practice, the Freedom Mantra?" I asked.

"With this practice, the soul finds freedom. Even if you practice the mantra for a few moments, you will embrace freedom in those few moments. The path to freedom, through this practice, is gradual.

Let me explain this to you with the analogy of a coin.

For a common man, a coin has two facets—heads and tails. Head is attachment, excitement, success, or happiness. Tail is repulsion, boredom, failure, and sorrow. The common man toggles between the head and tail of life.

For a Free Soul, a coin has three facets—head, tail, and the edge. This edge is the third path, a new aspect of life. This third path is free from the dualities of life. The Free Soul lives on the edge.

Free Souls do everything required in the world but are not affected by pain or gain, profit or loss, suffering, or happiness. They understand that duality is a part of life and embrace life on the edge.

The inspiration for a Free Soul—to get up in the morning and get going with life—is to embrace freedom.

And there is limitless joy in freedom."

He replied.

This brought jitters through my body; what a great way to live life. I was blown away by the idea itself. I could see the mental picture of the coin—attachment on one side, repulsion on the other, and a Free Soul walking on the edge, rotating the coin without reward-seeking actions.

* * *

The old man was making some sense. Yet, it was difficult for me to comprehend this thought of doing duties and not being attached to rewards. After all, all my life, I was in search of success, fame, and money. My desires were my strength—and this philosophy was questioning my belief system.

After all, it's the desires that keep us alive. If I am not attached to my desires, how will I give the best to my work? If I am not with my desires, how will I get inspired to get up in the morning and get going with life? I had doubts, doubts, and more doubts.

Hence, my next set of questions was a deep dive into the Freedom Mantra.

Work and the Freedom Mantra

"I do my duties free from rewards."

He repeated the Freedom Mantra one more time. And surprisingly, I also repeated the mantra in my mind.

"If I don't have any desires in my life, how can I move forward in life?" I asked.

"We change the direction of our desires. We transform the desires into goals. Attachments-repulsions fuel desires. However, goals are free from attachments-repulsions.

Goals help us move forward in life. Free Souls energize the goals but are not attached or repelled by its rewards.

It is the desire to get the rewards that creates the energy of attachments-repulsions, happiness-sorrow, success-failure, and so on. Free Souls dissolve this energy by focusing on their goals and defocusing from its rewards."

He replied.

"Why are goals important in the practice of Freedom Mantra?" I asked.

"Life without direction goes nowhere. If you come on crossroads, the road that you select to move forward will depend on your destination, on your goals. However, if you don't have a goal, you will select any road. A person with a goal might commit ten mistakes, but a person without a goal would commit a hundred mistakes.

If you want something in your life, your intellect should say, I want it one hundred percent. There should be clarity about where you are going. And, your goals should always align with your duties.

Another great benefit of goals is that it helps you develop a routine. And, routines are essential in the practice of the Freedom Mantra."

He replied.

"Why are routines essential in this practice?" I asked.

"If you have an outer life that is well ordered, your inner life will be calmer. And Freedom Mantra teaches us to work with a calm mind. Routines eliminate distraction and help the mind to focus on the present moment. Through Routines, the mind stops running in multiple directions.

When the outer life is routine based, then the inner energies are in order. And, you can use these energies to complete the tasks for achieving your goal. However, when your outer life is out of order, all your energies will be wasted in fixing the unessential.

Routines develop concentration. Concentration builds will power. Will power strengthen decisions. Decisions lead to our goals. Learn to give sustained focus, longer hours, and complete dedication to your tasks and activities. The more you are routine oriented, the faster you will reach towards your goals.

Routines blossom creativity. Routines bring clarity. Routines quiet the mind. Routines help us reach our goals. And above all, Routines help us practice the Freedom Mantra."

He replied.

"If I don't focus on my rewards. How will I accomplish my goals?" I asked.

"We accomplish our goals through decisions. To achieve our goals, we decide to achieve them. We keep working on our decision without being attached to the rewards.

The root word for decision in Latin translates to—cutting off the unwanted choices. And that is exactly what we do, we cut off the unwanted choices and accept a single choice. This single choice is our goal. Now, no matter what the hurdle is—pain, struggle, or getting out of our comfort zone—we work towards that goal without being attached to its rewards.

We give the power to our decision and work on our goals. We do not give the power to the rewards of our goals."

He replied.

"My rewards propel me to work. If there are no rewards, why should I work?" I asked.

"There are two paths that propel us to work—Inspiration and Motivation. Inspiration propels us to work because of our inner nature. Motivation propels us to work because we are seeking rewards.

Free Souls choose the path of inspiration to work. Rewards do not drive them. Their inner nature drives them. They work because it's their duty to work. They consider work as worship."

He replied.

"What should I do to get inspired and achieve my goals?" I asked.

"You have to identify your 'why'. If your 'why' is strong, you will automatically get inspired.

'Why' is the reason you do something. When you keep energizing your why, the inspiration will come easily.

Let's say you want to write a book; then you keep asking yourself—why do I want to write the book?

Your 'why' could be to help others or could be driven by your inner nature. Whatever your "why" is, the more it gets stronger, the more inspired you will be.

Your 'why' is the cause of your actions. You energize the 'why' to get your inspiration. Your goals stem from your 'why'.

With a stronger 'why', you will get inspired to do your duties. And then, you can use the Freedom Mantra to strengthen the 'how' of your work."

He replied.

"What is the 'How' of work?" I asked.

"Your 'how' is the way you work on your goals. Freedom Mantra teaches you the 'how' of work, that is, to work with complete dedication; without being attached to the outcome.

Therefore, when you write a book, it will become a masterpiece automatically—because your work is free from attachments-repulsions and reward-seeking actions."

He replied.

"I struggle with focus; can the Freedom Mantra help me focus on my work?" I asked.

"The charm of Freedom Mantra is that it helps us develop focus. The moment we are free from rewards, the mind becomes centered, it stops running in multiple directions, and it becomes completely relaxed.

In this relaxed state, the power of attention increases. and we can focus on the task at hand."

He replied.

"Even if I am not working for rewards, I should have some interest in my work. How can I work without interest?" I asked.

"I am not suggesting that you work without interest. In reality, your inner nature will propel you to work in your area of interest. You cannot stop it.

Freedom Mantra is not about 'Un-Interested Actions'. Freedom Mantra is about 'Dis-Interested Actions'.

These two words have different meanings in the English Dictionary.

When we are un-interested in any work, we work without attention—and—we are apathetic, bored, and separated from our work.

When we are dis-interested in any work, we work with attention—and—we are impartial, neutral, and devoted to our work.

When you learn to remove un-interested actions and learn to practice dis-interested actions, you will master the Freedom Mantra."

He replied.

"How do I know if my duty is right or wrong?" I asked.

"Right or wrong is a relative phenomenon. You have to ask your conscience, the Divine inside you, to guide you towards the right path. However, Duties that help serve humanity and are free from personal rewards are always right. This is the compass to select duties.

Also, with this practice, you develop the skill of differentiating between the pleasurable and the preferable. Most of the times, life presents us two choices—one is the pleasurable choice, and the other is the preferable choice. The pleasurable choice will give you immediate gratification but will harm you in the future. The preferable choice will be painful in the beginning but will give you satisfaction in the future.

When the Freedom Mantra sinks into your mind-body complex, you will choose the preferable over the pleasurable. "

He replied.

“I get bored very easily. Can the Freedom Mantra help me deal with my boredom?” I asked.

“The mind gets bored because it is always looking for excitement. However, Free Souls treat alike boredom and excitement, because when they do that—they find joy.

Free Souls find Inaction in Action and Action in Inaction. This simple approach keeps them in a joyous state all the time.

Let me explain.

Free Souls do not consider work or activity as drudgery. When they are busy, they enjoy their work, because they are working for the joy of work and not for the rewards of work. ‘Work’ becomes ‘No Work’ for them. Hence, they experience joy. This is called Inaction in Action.

Similarly, when they have minimal work, they embrace the lack of activity. In these situations, they enjoy the simple act of breathing or contemplating the Freedom Mantra. In these quiet moments, their thoughts are not seeking rewards. Hence, they experience joy. This is called Action in Inaction.

For a Free Soul—monday morning is as joyful as friday evening, workplace is as joyful as home, and work is as joyful as vacation. “

He replied.

"My work demands lots of hours and is very stressful. Can the Freedom Mantra, help me manage my stress? "I asked.

"Stress is a product of the mind, that is transmitted all over the body. Stress is produced because the mind is always working for rewards, because the mind is always seeking something, and because the mind is always anxious about the end result.

However, when the mind starts looking at work as duties and not as rewards—it finds peace. By doing duties free from rewards, the mind stops creating stress.

This is one of the most beneficial side effects of the Freedom Mantra."

He replied.

"Can you give me an example of someone who practices the Freedom mantra at work?" I asked.

"The best practitioners of Freedom Mantra are the nurses, the caregivers, and the nannies of the world. They look at the patients, old people, or children—as if they were their bloodline. They take care of them from their hearts and do their duties with total dedication.

However, when they complete their duties and move on to the next person—they leave their attachments behind. They take care of the next person with equal dedication.

Their work is selfless. And, Freedom Mantra teaches us the art of selfless work."

He replied.

"What is the difference between Free Souls versus renunciates who discard worldly duties?" I asked.

"Renunciation is the withdrawal from action; Freedom is all about action. Free Souls do their job, their dharma, and their duties— with detachment. On the contrary, renunciates sit in a cave to meditate.

Free Souls are not indifferent to the world around them. On the contrary, they perform actions that create a better future.

Free Souls neither suppress nor react. They realize that joy is nothing but observing the ups and downs of life with a resolute mind.

Free Souls give their heart, mind, and intellect to every action they undertake—but—they are completely detached from the outcome of their actions.

Free Souls maintain equanimity towards the outcome of their actions—they are okay if they get what they want and are okay if they don't.

Free Souls choose actions that benefit society—their actions are not based on selfish motives.

Free Souls choose work that aligns with their nature—they are not influenced by what others are doing.

Free Souls focus on their journey and not on their destination—they enjoy the process of doing things.

This might sound very simple, but it takes courage to become a Free Soul. And it needs practice. A lot of practice."

He replied.

* * *

I must admit that at this point, I got a feeling, deep down inside my gut, that I have found the answers to my problems. I might eventually embrace freedom. All I had to do was to practice the mantra diligently.

But the old man had more to offer.

Life and the Freedom Mantra

"The meaning of life is to live—to live in complete freedom. Life is beyond the dualities of birth or death, happiness or sorrow, and excitement or boredom."

He said.

And then he recited the Freedom Mantra.

"I do my duties free from rewards."

He did not miss a beat to remind me about the mantra and its words. By this time, the mantra and its words got registered in my memory.

"Can the Freedom Mantra— help me deal with my negative emotions like fear, anger, and guilt?" I asked.

"Attachments-Repulsions to the never-ending desires is the root cause of all negative emotions.

Fear arises because we are anxious about losing our rewards. But, through the act of not seeking rewards, we are not fearful about losing our rewards. We understand that loss or gain are a part of life. This dissolves the fear completely.

Anger arises when our desires are not fulfilled. But through the act of not seeking rewards, we are okay if things happen our way, and we are okay if they don't. We understand that success or failure is a part of life. This dissolves the anger completely.

Guilt arises when we think that we have done something wrong. But through the act of doing our duties, with complete dedication, we are not guilty if the outcome is not favorable. We understand that we did our best in the given situation. This dissolves the guilt completely.

Free Souls have been following this mantra to deal with negative emotions for over five thousand years. "

He replied.

"**I often get into arguments with my friends and family. Can the Freedom Mantra help me here?** "I asked.

"Freedom Mantra helps us develop the skill of letting go of our attachments-repulsions and reward-seeking actions. In other words, this is nothing but having—**zero expectations.**

When we have zero expectations from our friends and family, we can interact with them without the burden of getting offended. After you develop the art of having zero expectations, you will realize that in most situations, you were getting offended because of your expectations from others.

However, with the practice of Freedom Mantra, you are free to choose to argue or not to argue."

He replied.

"I am unable to forgive people. Can this mantra help me practice forgiveness? "I asked.

"Forgiveness is the art of letting go of resentment against a specific person. After your practice develops, you will see that you were unable to forgive people because they did not meet your expectations. Once you let go of that expectation and that attachment-repulsion, which was holding you, you will see people with a clear mind.

And in this elevated state of mind, you will be able to forgive that person because you will understand that forgiveness is for your inner peace and has nothing to do with the other person."

He replied.

"What happens to the person who has completely eliminated attachments-repulsions and is free from rewards? I asked.

"Attachments-Repulsions propel us to seek rewards. Once we are free from them, we are in direct connection with the source of existence, the Divine.

As we stabilize in this state, we start receiving the Grace of Divine. And through this Divine Grace, all sorrows are eliminated, and we find eternal peace. "

He replied.

"Attachment to good people, good things, and good situations creates positive energy. Why should I let it go?" I asked.

"You are right. Attachment to good people, things, and situations creates positive energy. Similarly, repulsion to bad people, things, and situations creates negative energy.

Do not get attached to positive energy and do not get repelled by negative energy—because—becoming free from attachments-repulsions creates the energy of Grace.

Positive or negative energy is temporary. They come and go. However, grace energy lasts as long as you are out of attachments-repulsions. It's in your hands. It brings peace, bliss, and freedom with it.

We receive grace energy, not because we deserve it, and not because of our good Karmas. We receive grace energy because we are on a new path, on a new dimension, and on a new channel. And grace overflows in this new channel.

With the energy of grace, we find the best goals, the best course of action, and the best path. All the suffering ends through this energy of grace, and life finds meaning and direction."

He replied.

"Why should I be quiet towards evil people, evil things, and evil situations? " I asked.

"I am not telling you to be quiet against evil. I am telling you to take action against evil without the energy of repulsion.

Evil and Good both exist in the world. Pain and Pleasure both exist in the world. Suffering and Joy both exist in the world.

Understand that evil, pain, and suffering are the consequences of past Karmas. They are here to teach us something. They are here to elevate us to a higher level.

Hence when you see evil, pain, or suffering—do the following three things.

Firstly, understand that it exists. It is the way the world works. The key is to be okay from its existence, that is, to be mentally free from this bad reward.

Secondly, with the understanding of its existence, let go of that repulsion around that evil, pain, or suffering. This will help you comprehend with clarity.

Thirdly, after dissolving the clouds of repulsion, take action to fix that evil, pain, or suffering. Utilize the means and tools available at your disposal. Or take a resolve to fix it.

And, because you have removed the negative energy, you have an unlimited source of grace energy that assists you, in your actions, to curb evil.

The key here is that you don't have to be agitated by that evil, pain, or suffering. Instead, you have to work to fix it without your repulsions. "

He replied.

Understanding the Mind

"The mind can be your best friend or worst enemy. The mind can become your best friend when you understand how it works. Because with a clear understanding of the mind, you can reprogram it with the Freedom Mantra—**I do my duties free from rewards."**

He said.

"Can you explain how the mind works?" I asked.

"Before you understand how the mind works, you have to understand how Karma works.

The law of Karma, or the law of cause and effect, is simple. It's the natural law that confirms that our future lies in our hands. We reap what we sow.

The present moment is the child of the past. Our present life—all that we have encountered and experienced—results from the actions we have taken in the past.

The future is the child of the present. Our future completely depends on the actions we take in the present moment. The interesting fact is that the present moment gives us the option to choose our future."

He replied.

"At times, we have to take harsh actions. Do we create bad Karma with harsh actions?" I asked.

"In the world we live in, we consider physical and verbal actions very important. But in truth, the intention behind our actions—what we think, what we feel, and what we perceive—are the real factors that trigger Karma.

Beating a person or being rude to someone verbally may seem to cause bad Karma, but the intention behind the act has to be considered. A mother might spank her child, or a father might scold his kid, but they choose these actions to benefit the children in the long term. This does not produce bad Karma.

However, if the mother is spanking her child because she is fueled with anger that is driven by her failures—then she creates bad Karma. Similarly, if the father is scolding the child to release any frustration of his office work—then he creates bad Karma.

It is the motivation behind the action that becomes the key ingredient. Before any action, a person feels a sense of attachment-repulsion of the event. This attachment-repulsion is triggered because the mind is either seeking a positive reward or a negative reward. The Karma that creates our future is the motivation behind the action. "

He replied.

"What needs to be done, to see our choices clearly and henceforth make better decisions?" I asked.

"Every decision is an internal battle fought on the battlefield of the mind. Every decision we make creates our future. Hence making good decisions is an essential facet of our lives.

If our feelings overpower our decisions, we will end up making the wrong decisions. Hence, we should never make a decision when we are too happy or too sad, because, in these two states, the mind is out of balance.

When the energy of rewards (attachments-repulsions) is produced, again and again, moment after moment, it gains intensity—and we start reacting in a habitual pattern to this energy. Thereafter our inner vision gets cluttered because these unwanted energies cloud the mind.

The only way out is to break this habitual pattern.

To make good decisions—you have to see people, things, and situations clearly—as they are.

To see clearly—you have to remove the unwanted energy—of attachments-repulsions.

He replied.

"Can you explain, with an example, of letting go of attachments-repulsions?" I asked.

"Letting go of attachments-repulsions can be explained through the example of a monkey.

A monkey trainer keeps a banana in a jar, that has a very narrow opening, to trap the monkey.

The monkey puts his hand inside the jar, holds the banana, but is unable to take out the banana with his hands. He thinks that his hand is stuck in the jar, and he is trapped.

However, the monkey just needs to let go of the banana, and he will be free. The moment he frees himself from the banana, he converts himself from a monkey to a monk.

Similarly, we humans are stuck with our attachments and repulsions. The reward from banana, in the story above, is nothing but our attachments-repulsions. The moment we let them go, we free ourselves to embrace freedom, and this freedom empowers our inner vision to see clearly."

He replied.

"What is the method to remove the unwanted energy of rewards (attachments-repulsions) from the mind, so that we can see clearly?" I asked.

"The reward seeking energy of attachments-repulsions is removed by **'Letting go through Contemplation'**. You should practice this whenever your mind gets attached or repelled by an object (People, Places, Situations) in the outer world.

In addition to that, practice this method two times every day. If you are committed to daily practice, you will eliminate this reward seeking energy from your mind. Just like you clean your body everyday by taking a shower, develop a habit to clean your mind everyday by eliminating the unwanted energy of rewards (attachments-repulsions).

Letting go through Contemplation:

The idea behind this method is that, you hold on and follow the thought below—

I free from attachments-repulsions.

In this thought, use the word 'free' as a verb, as an actionable item, as an act of freeing from the rewards. We use attachments-repulsions because it the root thought of all rewards.

And then, close your eyes, take a few deep breaths, and observe your mind. Now, identify the object in the outer world that creates attachment or repulsion. Once the object is identified—accept the idea to be free from this object, and simultaneously, drop the energy of attachments-repulsions around it. It's a mental action, just let go of the energy.

Keep doing this until the mind is completely free from rewards (attachments-repulsions).

During the initial stages of the practice, while contemplating, you might find it very challenging to accept the idea of dropping the energy of attachment or repulsion. Sometimes, the thought that you are dealing with can be very emotional, and the mind will resist all the way. The mind will create multiple scenarios and stories to stop letting go.

In these moments, you will have to identify and acknowledge the **worst-case-scenario.** Once you acknowledge that the worst can happen—the mind becomes free. It becomes free of both good rewards and bad rewards. And the attachments-repulsions fizzle out on their own.

This process of Letting go trains the mind to see with clarity. Understand this—the untrained mind is the cause of your clouded choices, and the trained mind is the cause of your clear decisions."

He replied.

"How does the untrained mind work?" I asked.

"Whenever the five senses (sight, hearing, taste, touch, and smell) experience people, things, or situations—the mind analyses the experience and then acts on it.

If the mind perceives the experience as good; it wants to hold onto it and magnify it. On the other hand, if the mind analyses the experience as bad; it wants to discard it and run away from it. This analysis is done in a split second, and most of the time, we are not aware of it.

Over the years, we have been reacting in an automated way—at the mercy of our mind. When we like something, we react with excitement, pleasure, and happiness. And when we dislike something, we react with anger, fear, and worry. We react blindly because our actions are always seeking rewards.

He replied.

"Can you explain, the untrained mind, with an example?" I asked.

"There is an old story about a horse and a man traveling on an endless road. The horse was galloping quickly, and it seemed that the rider had somewhere important to go. The rider was restless and was running out of time.

Another man who watched them from the sidewalk shouted and asked, 'Where are you going?'

The rider replied, 'I don't know; ask the horse.'

The horse in the story symbolizes the untrained mind. We put ourselves at the mercy of our mind. The horse controls our life and takes us wherever it wants to."

He replied.

"How can we train the untrained mind?" I asked.

"You have to reprogram the mind through the intellect. Our intellect governs our mind, hence if the intellect tells the mind to alter the process—the mind will follow its command. There is a method to activate the intellect to reprogram the mind. I will talk about the method in a moment (Next chapter in the book).

Before you learn how to train the mind, you have to understand what needs to be done, to train the mind.

"What needs to be done to train the mind?" I asked.

You have to alter the behavior of the mind. And this change should happen at the moment when the mind starts analyzing the experience.

When you are in the state of perception, let go of the energy of rewards (attachments-repulsions). The moment you let go of the energy of rewards, you can see the situation as it is. This helps in taking better actions.

And then do the duty free from rewards. The moment you are not seeking rewards, you give the best to your actions.

When the mind is trained to respond free from rewards—you are free from the bondage of Karma. You are okay if you get the desired result. You are okay if you don't get the desired result.

This simple alteration in your behavior pattern changes the cycle of Karma in your favor. "

He replied.

"Can you explain, with an example, on altering the states of mind?" I asked.

"Let me explain this through addictions. Everyone has experienced addiction once in this life. On one hand, people might become addicted to alcohol, smoking, or eating. And on the other hand, they might become addicted to spirituality, religion, or fanaticism. So how do we find the path to free ourselves?

Freedom Mantra helps us here.

Let's say you are addicted to smoking, and you intend to quit smoking. Whenever the urge to smoke a cigarette arrives, pause for a few moments.

And, then, let go of your attachment-repulsions for the rewards of smoking. When the clouds of rewards are removed, you can see the situation clearly—to question yourself—why am I smoking?

And, then, smoke, but without clinging to the rewards of smoking. This is a mental action, you smoke physically, but mentally you are free from the rewards of smoking. Every cigarette you smoke will make you realize that this addiction is all about habits.

When you are not restless about the rewards of smoking—you will have a simple choice, i.e., to smoke or not to smoke. And then, you can make a decision, to quit smoking or continue smoking.

When you do this regularly, you can eradicate your addiction to smoking. It might not happen on the first day, but you will get there by practice and will power."

He replied.

Intellect Reprograms the Mind

The old man paused for a few moments—the busiest airport in the world became a silent desert. I could not hear any announcements or any background noise. I felt complete bliss at that moment as if life was visiting me.

There was a feeling of peace inside my entire being. My gut was telling me that I had found the right path, that my restlessness would disappear soon, and that life would not be the same from that moment onward.

He then wrote a formula on his boarding pass and asked me to internalize it. I looked at the formula repeatedly.

Here it is.

Freedom = Do your Duties free from rewards.

As I tried to internalize it, I started thinking about the struggle in this practice. The formula for freedom was right in front of me, but I had to climb a huge mountain to become a practitioner of freedom.

"This is not an easy path." I said.

"The practice of Freedom Mantra is like a poison in the beginning. However, when the mantra becomes your second nature, this poison brings the nectar of peace.

If you don't know swimming, you will resist all the way to get inside the water. But, when you learn swimming slowly and steadily, you will start enjoying every moment in the water.

Freedom comes with hard work. You will have to discover freedom on your own. I can only show you the path. You will have to put in the effort and energy.

Practice the Freedom Mantra for every situation in your life. And you will become a Free Soul. However, have patience, this will take time."

He said.

"I understand that Freedom Mantra is the answer to life. However, when I go on with my life, I will forget the mantra—what is the way out?" I asked.

"The way out is to remember the mantra all the time. But before I teach the method to remember the mantra—

Understand this:

The goal is to free the mind from rewards (attachments-repulsions, success-failure, happiness-sorrow, and so on). And then do our duties with complete dedication.

When the object of our desire or hatred keeps presenting itself—again and again in the mind—the reward seeking energies are created. The mind gets obsessed with the object we are seeking or discarding, and this obsession leads to reward-seeking actions.

To break this habit, you have to learn to replace the thoughts of the mind. Hence whenever the object of desire or hatred shows up, replace it with Freedom Mantra.

And when the mind sees that it can still work on the goal, without clinging on the object of desire or hatred, it does not create attachments-repulsions and reward-seeking actions."

He replied.

"What is the method to remember the Freedom Mantra?" I asked.

"The method is called **'Remember through Repetition'**. The method uses the intellect to gain mastery of the mind. It is the intellect that controls the mind, and we use the intellect to reprogram the mind through repetition.

Remember through Repetition:

Close your eyes, take a few deep breaths, and think about the Freedom Mantra. Keep repeating the mantra— I do my duties free from rewards—again and again, inside your mind. You don't have to speak them out. It's a mental repetition. Do this the first thing in the morning, and the last thing before sleeping.

Another way to practice 'Remember through Repetition' is to write down the mantra—I do my duties free from rewards—108 times regularly. This will sink the mantra into your soul. We write it 108 times because there are 108 energy points within the body, and the concept is to embrace these energy points. You don't have to think about the energy points; it's just a thought in the mind.

And then use the Freedom Mantra with your endeavors with life."

He replied.

"How do I use the Freedom Mantra with my endeavors?" I asked.

"Use the idea behind the Freedom Mantra in your day to day life. Every activity that you do; infuse it with the Freedom Mantra. The mantra should be present with you every moment, for every endeavor, and in every breath.

Initially, the mind will throw challenges to accept the idea of doing your duties free from rewards. However, through will power, force your mind to focus on the work and not on its rewards.

Sometimes, the thought that you are dealing with can be very emotional, and the mind will resist all the way. The mind will create multiple scenarios and stories to start seeking rewards. In these moments, you will have to identify the **worst-case-scenario.** And then, acknowledge the worst-case-scenario. And finally, through courage, do your duties, while recognizing the worst-case-scenario.

It takes courage and will power to do the duties free from rewards. But once you get the hang of it; your life will find permanent joy."

He replied.

"Why do I have to repeat the mantra, in my mind?" I asked.

"As I mentioned earlier, our intellect governs our mind. Through repetition, we ignite the intellect to take action.

Understand this through a prism that has four levels. The bottom level of the prism is the five senses; the first level is the mind; the second level is the intellect; the topmost level of the prism is the soul. The soul is the master.

In a state of perfect harmony—the soul guides the intellect, the intellect guides the mind, and the mind guides the five senses (sight, smell, hearing, touch, and taste.)

However, for most of us, when we experience something through the five senses, the mind develops attachments-repulsions towards that experience. Either we want the same experience again and again, or we don't want to experience the situation. The mind is the creator of these attachments-repulsions, happiness-sorrow, success-failure, and so on.

And, because the intellect governs the mind—If

the intellect is strong enough to tell the mind to take a particular action—the mind will follow its command.

Repeating the mantra, activates the intellect—to reprogram the mind—and the mind follows the command of the intellect."

He replied.

"Can you explain about Intellect and Mind through another example?" I asked.

"Let me explain this with a chariot that is designed to operate with five horses. The charioteer controls the ropes tied to the mouth of these horses. And you are sitting, as a passenger, in the chariot, behind the charioteer.

The five horses are your five senses (sight, smell, hearing, touch, and taste), the ropes combined is your mind, the charioteer is your intellect, and the passenger is the soul.

All you have to do, as a passenger (Soul), is to instruct the charioteer (Intellect) to lead you on the right path. And the charioteer (Intellect) will program the ropes (Mind) accordingly. And eventually, the five horses (Five senses) will behave as per the guidance of the soul.

When you keep repeating the Freedom Mantra, the mantra becomes your natural response in any situation. And whenever the mind develops attachments-repulsions or rewards seeking actions—the intellect will stop it with the Freedom Mantra. It will become your natural habit.

This practice of Freedom Mantra is the habit-energy; it's our spiritual muscle. With regular practice, we make this spiritual muscle stronger and stronger. If you have this energy, you have cracked the code of life."

He replied.

"Understand this—Learn the habit of instructing the mind, and simultaneously, unlearn the habit of taking instructions from the mind."

He added.

* * *

I understood the why of my problems—clinging on rewards.

I understood who creates the problems—the mind.

I understood who controls the mind—the intellect.

I understood how to solve the problem—activate the intellect.

I understood what needs to be done—reprogram the mind with the Freedom Mantra.

The path ahead was clear—to do my duties free from rewards. But I was about to learn a secret that could fuel the power of the Freedom Mantra.

The Secret, Giving it to God

"The practice of Freedom Mantra brings immediate liberation. The Freedom Mantra is complete in itself—**I do my duties free from rewards.**

However, you can fuel the power of the Freedom Mantra through a secret."

He said.

"Can you share the secret to fuel the power of the Freedom Mantra?" I asked.

"To learn this secret, you should have faith in the Divine. If you are an atheist and don't have faith in God, then you may continue with the Freedom Mantra without applying this secret.

However, if you believe in Divine—the secret is to Give it to God.

Every morning, surrender your actions and rewards to God. If you have an alter in your house, do it there.

If you don't, just surrender in a quiet place. It's a mental surrender, you don't have to offer anything physical but mentally offer everything you have (actions and rewards), to God. And during the day, keep doing your duties, free from rewards, as a worship to God."

He replied.

"What happens when I give my actions and rewards to God?" I asked.

"Giving our Actions and Rewards to God is the act of dissolving our pride and developing an attitude that whatever we are doing is for God. We are just an instrument in his hands.

Giving our Actions and Rewards to God is a mental process in which we give our mind to God. It's an action to align our will with the divine will.

Giving our Actions and Rewards to God is a form of sacrifice that purifies our heart and dissolves the egoic I. Through offering our actions and rewards to God, we understand that it is God that is working through us.

Giving our Actions and Rewards to God helps us get rid of attachments-repulsions, because, we free ourselves from the burden of our desires.

Giving our Actions and Rewards to God fuels the practice of Freedom Mantra with divine wisdom, divine love, and divine grace. The more we give to God, the more our actions get transformed to purify our mind and benefit the society. "

He replied.

"I pray every day to God. Is it not the same thing?" I asked.

"The majority of humanity prays to God so that God can fulfill their desires. This form of prayer creates attachments-repulsions because people start clinging to the object of their desire.

However, what I am suggesting is the complete opposite of the 'prayer of asking'. I am suggesting that you offer everything you have to God. It's an offering in your inner world. It's a mental offering. It's a submission."

He replied.

"Are you suggesting that I stop praying?" I asked.

"No, I am not asking you to stop praying. I am asking you to change the way you pray. Don't ask God for this or that. Don't give him the options available to achieve your goals. Instead, pray to God to lead your way. And then offer your actions and rewards to him.

By giving it to God, we develop a strong belief, strong faith, and strong assurance—that God is leading our way. Even if there is pain and suffering in God's path, we accept that it is the right path. We believe that eventually, this path will liberate us because it is from God.

When we give it to God—we treat alike the desirable and not desirable, and we trust that God is leading our way."

He replied.

"How do I find out the will of God?" I asked.

"Until you have reached a state of permanent freedom—it is difficult to know the will of God. However, the Freedom Mantra helps to find the right direction.

Whenever you are seeking direction or guidance from God—sit down for a few moments, practice 'Letting Go through Contemplation', and purify your mind from attachments-repulsions. There should be no craving or aversion in the mind. The mind should be free from rewards.

In this state, you enable the flow of Divine Grace. And then, you automatically discover the right direction, in the silence of your heart."

He replied.

* * *

At this moment, I had a clear understanding of the Freedom Mantra. But I wanted to learn more; I wanted to get inside his mind; hence, I started asking questions on each and every word in the Freedom Mantra.

I Do

Well, you know, whatever is the stage of our life, the drive to grow should never stop. We need to explore the inner world along with the outer world. However, in reality, the outer world is just a reflection of the inner world.

And the best way to explore the inner world and the outer world is through the practice of Freedom Mantra—**I do my duties free from rewards.**"

He said.

I was listening with complete attention. He was making so much sense. All my life, I have been focused on my outer world, neglecting my inner world. Now, was the time to change the game of life.

"Can you talk more about the part 'I Do' in the Freedom Mantra?" I asked.

"When you say—I do my duties free from rewards—the word 'do' encapsulates a critical message.

Let me explain. When you say—I do—you have to do your duties. You cannot procrastinate. Even if you don't feel like doing your work, you have to get up in the morning and do your duties. You cannot be attached to inaction or no work.

Life will bring you into a situation, wherein you will find your duties painful, laborious, and non-exciting. However, the key to master the Freedom Mantra, is to keep doing your duties.

For example, my job is all about travelling. I travel for six months in a year. I sacrifice a lot for my job. I don't see my wife and son for many days. At times, this is very tough because I miss out on so many important events in our life. But I cannot shy away from doing my duties. Whatever happens, I have to travel—to do my duties.

I have understood that if I do not do my work and stay back in my home—I will hinder the flow of life.

Hence, I do my job with all sincerity giving my one hundred percent to my tasks. This simple practice of doing the duties, by giving complete attention to them—is a source of liberation for the mind. When we are completely involved in something, the mind stops worrying. "

He replied.

"So, what you are saying is that how we work is directly related to how the mind sees the world?" I asked.

"If you give one hundred percent to your work, your mind will start enjoying life. Many evolved souls have called this technique—to live in the present moment. The practice is to fall in love with your work.

We can experience, enjoy, and appreciate life only at the crossroads of the here and now. The biggest suffering in life happens, when in the present moment, you want to be someplace else. You can transform your suffering when you completely surrender into the present moment.

Also, time loses its grip in the present moment. The past and the future become one when you are truly in the moment. The present moment, when experienced in totality, transcends time and makes our fears and anxieties disappear.

Have you ever wondered why younger kids are always happy? It is because they don't have a past and they cannot think about their future. They are always in the moment. And when they join kindergarten, all the worries start flowing—anxiety about homework, fear of losing friends, and, above all, the stress of managing the expectations of parents.

Hence my friend, learn to give one hundred percent to your duties, for it will help you stay in the present moment and will bring peace and joy."

He replied.

"What are the other benefits of giving one hundred percent to our work?" I asked.

"This practice, of giving your complete attention to the task at hand, develops the skill of mono-tasking. For example, right now, I am talking to you—and—doing nothing else.

In today's world, people find it very difficult to do one thing at a time. They are always multitasking—eating food while sending e-mails, chatting with multiple people simultaneously on instant messengers, or talking with their spouse while updating their social media status.

However, in reality, when you are in the moment, completely dedicated to the task at hand, you become more effective.

Mono-tasking or being in the moment also activates the subconscious mind. It helps with intuitive decisions. Many great innovators have made discoveries when they were not thinking, in the moments when they were completely engrossed in the here and now."

He replied.

"What if there is too much confusion, lack of direction, and chaos while doing my duties. How do I manage that? "I asked.

"Success in practicing Freedom Mantra is achieved when a person is peaceful in total chaos and also peaceful in zero activity. The Freedom Mantra is for a person of solitary lifestyle and also for a person of active lifestyle.

If the person of a solitary lifestyle reaches a big city full of traffic lights, cars, and pedestrians—and yet in this intense activity—is able to maintain calmness, that person has mastered the Freedom Mantra.

Similarly, if a person of active lifestyle reaches a forest, mountain, or village that is immensely quiet—and yet in this extreme solitude—is able to maintain calmness, that person has mastered the Freedom Mantra.

Freedom Mantra teaches us to do our duties in whatever situation we are placed in—without attachments-repulsions or reward-seeking actions."

He replied.

"Sometimes, in the midst of intense activity, my mind produces disturbing thoughts. These thoughts destroy my drive to work. Can the Freedom Mantra help me here? "I asked.

"Let me explain how the mind produces thoughts.

Because of our past actions or past Karmas, we create impressions and imprints in our subconscious mind. For example, if you got angry at someone in your adolescent years, and that event disturbed your psyche—you created an impression in your subconscious mind.

These impressions manifest themselves as thoughts in our conscious mind.

The impressions and thoughts are triggered when a similar event happens, or when the mind is attached to the rewards of your current activity. The manifested thoughts stay in the conscious mind for some moments, gain intensity because our psyche gets disturbed, and eventually go back into the subconscious mind as amplified impressions. It's a cycle, and we need to break the cycle—this process is called the purification of the mind.

We don't have to fight with the disturbing thoughts, because the more we fight, the more intense they get. The best way to deal with disturbing thoughts is that the moment we identify them, replace them with better thoughts. And there is no better thought than the Freedom Mantra.

Whenever a disturbing thought arises, remember the Freedom Mantra—Do your duties free from rewards. Remember that the rewards are the attachments-repulsions that have manifested as thoughts. And, when the mind understands that it does not have to cling to these disturbing thoughts, the thoughts lose their intensity. They get fizzled out and do not go back into the subconscious mind.

The more we practice, the more the mind gets purified, and starts producing beneficial thoughts."

He replied.

"My profession is very demanding, and sometimes I just give up." I said.

In any profession, we face challenges, and the mind starts procrastinating. As a writer, you might have faced challenges when the ideas won't come out. But then, if you write anyways and overcome laziness—you will find something meaningful in those tough sessions. The key is to show up for your work.

Freedom Mantra is not about running away from our goals and duties. On the contrary, it helps us to achieve our goals because we learn to give a hundred percent of our attention to them. "

He said.

My Duties

We can use our duties, our work, and our profession to purify the mind. This is achieved through the practice of the Freedom Mantra—**I do my duties free from rewards.**"

He said.

"Can you talk more about 'My Duties' in the Freedom Mantra?" I asked.

"Everyone has a calling; all we have to do is connect with it. When we are aligned with our duties, the entire universe starts working with us. This brings us in a state of flow.

The duties of our life have to align with the divine will and with the divine purpose. The divine uses our stage in life, our skills, and our strengths—to assign our duties.

To understand duties, you have to understand its two branches. The first one is how to identify the duties, and the second one is how to relate to the duties."

He replied.

"Earlier, you mentioned about identifying the duties. Are they that important?" I asked.

"Yes, identification of your duties and working on them is one of the key ingredients of the Freedom Mantra. I did speak to you about identifying your duties. But let me reiterate the idea, because, it will also help me explain the next idea—on how to relate with duties.

Duties are the tasks and activities that we need to do to accomplish the purpose of our life. For e.g., taking care of our family, doing our daily job, cultivating our talents, doing our daily chores. These are all our duties. In general, duties are of two types:

Obligatory Duties:

Our obligatory duties are duties that align with the stage of our life. These are the duties that have to be done, even if you don't like them. Every person goes through multiple stages in life. These stages can be broadly classified into four categories—childhood, young adult, middle age, and retired life. Each stage has a different set of obligatory duties.

Sometimes, we do not want to do our obligatory duties because we find then boring, tiresome, and thankless. For example, cleaning our house, or working at a job that is not gratifying. However, we should utilize these obligatory duties as a means to practice the Freedom Mantra. Because, when we keep doing these duties with complete dedication and free from rewards, we find peace and fulfillment.

Inborn Duties:

Inborn Duties are duties that help us express our inner being. Every person is born with a set of strengths, and every person is inclined towards specific areas of work. These two aspects build our nature and help us identify our Inborn Duties. This set of duties could be our daily job, could be our hobby, or could be our passion.

The inborn duties can never harm us because they are born along with us. They reflect our true nature."

He replied.

"And how should I relate to my duties?" I asked.

"Stop Serving yourself and Start Serving others.

It is very simple. We are unhappy because we are totally self-possessed. Our entire life is around me, me, and me. We are only concerned about making our lives better and finding happiness for ourselves.

However, when we serve others, we forget about ourselves. When the goal of our life is to help others find joy, we find our joy without any struggle. We find joy as a residue for helping others.

This technique is a therapy for the mind; it cleanses the heart and nourishes the soul. But remember, do it with a pure intention.

In reality, this technique helps us fulfill our passions, our dreams, and our purpose.

If anything, we do, is an act to serve others, it clarifies our mental delusions about success. Our passions, our dreams, and our purpose lose the sense of 'Me' when they are directed toward serving others.

This therapy will dissolve the attachment to your self-serving mind and will bring permanent joy to you."

He replied.

"I have not done much for society. Can you suggest where should I start?" I asked.

"If you want to become an expert in practicing the Freedom Mantra, you should start with dishwashing. This simple, dull, and boring task can teach a lot about serving others.

Also, give your hundred percent when you wash dishes—reducing the flow of water to the bare minimum, removing the grease from the plates with deep love, and finally putting the dishes in the dishwasher so that they can be used to feed tomorrow.

In fact, many other household tasks like cleaning, cutting vegetables, or organizing closets, can help us serve our family. The problem is that most of us consider these tasks to be boring, and hence we develop a lot of resistance around it. But we should learn to embrace them.

And then when you have learnt to serve your family, you can start serving humanity."

He replied.

Free From Rewards

"Look around the airport; you will see the movement of life in every corner. Servers are serving food in restaurants, and vendors are delivering their products, and janitors cleaning the restrooms. Everyone is involved in their daily duties. It is a reflection of the fact that life is all about work.

And work is the most efficient when done with the Freedom Mantra—**I do my duties free from rewards.**"

He said.

"Can you talk more about the part 'Free From Rewards' in the Freedom Mantra?" I asked.

"Being free from rewards is to let go attachments-repulsions, to treat alike happiness-sorrow, to treat alike gain-loss, to treat alike victory-defeat, and to treat alike excitement-boredom. When you are not seeking rewards, you work for the sake of duty, with the best of your abilities."

He replied.

“What happens when our actions are not seeking rewards?” I asked.

“Doing our duties free from rewards helps us purify the mind. The mind is clouded, foggy, and cannot see the truth because of attachments-repulsions. The more you are free; the more clarity you will have.

For example, in the court of law, if there is a jury that is attached or repelled by the accused, then the jury cannot make a correct judgement. The jury cannot see the truth because of preconceived notions. Similarly, to see the truth behind people, things, and situations—every human being needs to see without being influenced by rewards.”

He replied.

“Can you talk more about rewards?” I asked.

“As I mentioned earlier—rewards are created by our attachments-repulsions, our likes-dislikes, cravings-aversions, and so on.

However, freedom from rewards can be further classified into the following—being separated from the outcome of your actions, and not being influenced by the payoffs of your actions.

Outcomes are the results of your actions, and payoffs are the fruits of your actions. Outcome is your victory or defeat. Payoff is the good fruit or bad fruit. Both outcomes and payoffs are delivered after an action is completed.”

He replied.

"Can you give an example of being separated from the outcomes?" I asked.

"Let me explain about—separation from outcomes—through the profession of an eye surgeon.

While doing his duties, the eye surgeon has to separate himself from the outcomes completely. He should be okay if he does a successful surgery, and he should be okay if he does not. He has to be completely detached from his patients. This is the only way he can perform better.

However, if he has to operate his son, for eye surgery, then, the medical fraternity will not allow him to do the surgery. The reason is that he could be too attached to his son, and this attachment could hinder his performance.

The medical fraternity is correct—attachment to the outcome influences the quality of our work. Hence the only way out is to work with total separation from the outcomes."

He replied.

"Can you give an example of not being influenced by payoffs?" I asked.

"Let me explain about payoffs from my own life. Because the secret to my success is not in my payoff's, but my inner perspective of not clinging to my payoffs.

As an Investor, CEO, and a Billionaire, I have failed many times. I have lost millions of dollars. Those losses are also my payoff's. I have also made millions of dollars. These gains are also my payoff's.

But I do not cling to the losses or gains.

The essence of Freedom Mantra is to work. But the moment you get influenced by your payoff's—you are far far away from freedom."

"It is my goal to write books that help humanity. How can I do this being free from rewards?" I asked.

"As you keep contemplating the Freedom Mantra, you will learn to detach from the outcomes and the payoffs.

When you write the book, separate yourself from the outcome of the book. Understand that all you can do is work with devotion, on writing the book, as the outcome is not in your hands. But be careful, and never ever forget that—separation is from the outcomes, not from the work. Keep giving the best to your work.

Also, while writing the book, do not think about the payoffs. Do not get influenced by the payoffs. The payoffs should never be the inspiration factor to write the book. The inspiration factor to write the book should come from your 'why', the inner reason that propels you to write the book."

He replied.

"All my life, I have been focused on rewards. Your teachings are giving me a new perspective." I said

"There is nothing wrong with enjoying your good rewards or disapproving your bad rewards. The problem arises when you cling to them, when you get consumed with them, and when you become your rewards.

Life knocks us down many times, but then we get up and start working to fix things.

If the rewards are good—we work hard to make them better.

If the rewards are bad—we work hard to make them good.

So, in reality, we are always working.

The ultimate goal of every human being is to find happiness. But the truth is that happiness has an element of excitement attached to it. And when the excitement goes away, happiness also disappears.

Real happiness or Joy happens when we are at peace. And Joy is more profound when our experiences are without clinging to the rewards.

The secret of life is to rise above rewards. Once you understand that, you will find freedom."

He said.

Skills To Practice The Freedom Mantra

"The practice of Freedom Mantra is a thinking muscle. It takes will power and commitment to practice it. There will be an initial struggle in accepting the idea behind it. But after a few days, it becomes our second nature. Freedom Mantra is just like a space shuttle, it takes all the energy to leave planet earth, but once it's in the orbit, it works magically.

The key is to remember and apply the Freedom Mantra—**I do my duties free from rewards.**"

He said.

"Is there a set of skills that I can develop, to practice the Freedom Mantra?" I asked.

"There are many skills that can help you with the practice of Freedom Mantra. These skills help in eliminating attachments-repulsions and reward seeking behavior. Some of them are—minimalism, physical workout, and the food on your plate.

He replied.

"What is Minimalism?" I asked.

"Minimalism is an understanding that Less is More. All the great leaders who transformed humanity were minimalists. They had few belongings, few friends, and few needs.

Through minimalism, we learn to become content with what we have, and we do not seek for more. Less becomes More. Also, because our needs and wants are limited, we are not influenced by rewards. We understand that our drive and our inspiration to work is not because of the rewards; our drive to work comes from our 'why', the inner reason that propels us to do our work."

He replied

"How can physical workout help me practice the Freedom Mantra?" I asked.

"Our body stores our attachments-repulsions. You might have experienced that whenever people get happy or restless—they start moving some part of their body. It's an involuntary action. The reason is that our attachments-repulsions are expressing themselves through body movements.

I have been a runner for most of my life. And my running plays a significant role in my practice. It helps me let go of my attachments-repulsions.

While running, I mentally release the attachment-repulsions stored in my body. These attachments-repulsions are deeply rooted, and it takes time to let them go. But even a little progress on this path leads to liberation. You will experience this on your own when you start practicing."

He replied.

"I cannot run. Is there any other way?" I asked.

"You don't have to run to let go of the attachments-repulsions. In fact, any physical activity—dancing, hiking, yoga, cycling, aerobics, stretching—release the attachments and the repulsions from the body. You will have to regulate your daily schedule, to give time to physical workout.

Also, practice 'Remember through Repetition' method, right after the physical workout, because in those moments, the mind is clear and quiet.

He replied.

"Is there anything else that I need to do to assist my body, to be free from rewards?" I asked.

"You need to give enough rest to your body and follow its rhythms. You need to sleep for eight hours and get up before sunrise. You should align your body clock with planet earth's body clock.

Getting up before sunrise keeps the body happy. There is an old German proverb—Morning has gold in its mouth. Something magical happens before sunrise. The environment is peaceful, and the air is fresh. The mind is silent, and the thoughts are minimal. In these moments, we can use the intellect, to reprogram the mind, with the Freedom Mantra.

Do not touch your phone, do not read newspapers, and do not watch television in the morning hours. Just wash your face and practice 'Remember through Repetition' method of the Freedom Mantra. The morning hours assist us in remembering the mantra.

Keep practicing. It will work magically, and it will make you an expert in Freedom Mantra."

He replied.

"How can food help me practice the Freedom Mantra?" I asked.

"The body is a temple where the soul resides. We need to keep the temple clean, peaceful, and healthy. Food plays a vital role in creating attachments-repulsions. When the body gets contaminated with high energy foods or low energy foods, it makes our mind greedy, angry, attached, and repulsive.

Only a peaceful body can practice the Freedom Mantra.

Learn to nourish your body with peace. The more peace you have in your body, the fewer attachments-repulsions will be produced. You have to be very mindful of the type of food you put inside your body. "

He replied.

"What kind of foods are beneficial to eliminate the reward seeking actions?" I asked.

"Foods can be classified into three categories—pure energy, high energy, and low energy. Pure energy foods are fresh fruits and vegetables. High energy foods are foods that are too salty, too sugary, or too spicy. Low energy foods are land animals or stale foods.

Pure energy foods balance the mind; they help us eliminate attachments-repulsions. High energy foods make the mind overactive; they create greed and anger. Low energy foods make the mind inactive; they create laziness, dullness, and delusion.

He replied.

"Can you talk more about pure energy foods?" I asked.

"Pure foods are plants, vegetables, lentils, and any living organism that does not carry blood. However, there are some exceptions, like garlic and onions, because these two vegetables make the mind dull and foggy.

Even if you eat plants, you are killing life. The truth is that, in this world, life has to feed itself with life. However, plants and vegetables are foods that the human body can process very efficiently. On the flip side, the body takes a lot of time to process land animals."

He replied.

"What are the high energy foods?" I asked.

"If your food is cooked with excess spices, or is too salty, or has extra sugar—then it becomes high energy food. This kind of food makes the mind overactive, and the mind starts seeking more and more. High energy foods create unwanted attachments-repulsions."

He replied.

"What are the low energy foods?" I asked.

"Land animals are low energy foods. The human intestine is not designed to eat land animals. In fact, most of the animals that humans eat are vegetarian. The flesh is an energy field that stores emotions, burdens, and sufferings. And when we eat the flesh of land animals, we feed our body with that suffering.

Also, stale food, frozen food, and reheated food are low energy foods. If the food you eat is not freshly prepared, it loses its life force, and it makes the mind lazy and lethargic. "

He replied.

"These are tough choices. Can you suggest where should I start?" I asked.

"The key is to find a balance. In today's world, it is difficult to eat only pure energy foods. But you can choose to increase pure energy foods in your diet. And you can choose to decrease high energy and low energy foods from your diet. The choice is always yours.

But always remember this—**we become what we eat; because the mind is a direct reflection of what we eat.**"

He replied.

The Teacher, The Guru, The Guide

I wanted more from him. I was not sure if I could handle this secret of life on my own. I believe he read my mind, and his next sentence came to my rescue.

"The teacher always arrives when the seeker is ready. So, my dear friend, you will find someone to guide you whenever you are ready.

And that someone doesn't have to be a person—it could be a book, a friend, or life itself.

But remember that your real teacher is the Freedom Mantra—**I do my duties free from rewards.**"

He said.

"It will take time to master the Freedom Mantra." I said.

"The practice of Freedom Mantra is a gradual process. During the initial stages of your practice, you will go back and forth between the attached mind and the detached mind. It is not an overnight journey. It takes time and effort to develop the idea of being detached from the outcome.

But as you will see, even a little application of detachment will bring immediate joy.

As I said earlier:

'For a Free Soul, a coin has three facets—head, tail, and the edge.

Free Souls lives on the edge. Free Souls get rid of attachments-repulsions and reward-seeking actions.

They do everything required in the world but are not affected by pain or gain, profit or loss, suffering, or happiness. They understand that duality is a part of life and embrace life on the edge.

The inspiration for a Free Soul—to get up in the morning and get going with life—is to embrace freedom.

And there is limitless joy in freedom.'

Keep practicing the Freedom Mantra, and the truth will reveal itself.

He said.

"What is the meaning of freedom?" I asked.

"Freedom is to be without any conflict or resistance with our thoughts, emotions, or situations in life. And that is exactly what this practice does. It stops the conflict. It stops the resistance and brings us to a state of calmness.

Freedom is not any physical location inside the body. It is simply an anchor from where you see your life—the inner life and the outer life.

Freedom is the art of experiencing JOY, twenty-four by seven."

He replied.

"You have given me great knowledge. I am hopeful of finding freedom through it." I said.

"I have given you the knowledge. But Wisdom comes through practice. Wisdom has two components—knowing and believing. This knowledge will empower your knowing, but it's the practice that will empower your believing.

If you listen to a knowledgeable person or read a book, you do not experience the truth; you are told about the truth. But through the journey of the Freedom Mantra, you experience the truth and require no further explanation.

Hence, my friend, remember that is this is your journey. You have the tools, the knowledge, and the guidepost called Freedom Mantra. Now, it is all in your hands. If you decide to pursue this path—freedom is assured."

He said.

At this moment, when I looked outside, I was astonished. The clouds and rains had disappeared. The Sun was bright, and its rays were falling all over the airport. I felt like the universe had cleared my path, and was leading me towards freedom.

And then he indicated that he had to leave.

Now was time to say goodbye to the Monk, the Billionaire, the CEO, the Guru, the Guide, and the Teacher. I had gratitude flowing out of my heart. No words in my limited dictionary could help me express his generosity towards me.

And as soon as I approached him, he spoke with his peaceful smile.

"Enjoy the journey, my friend. Even a little progress on this path will lead you towards freedom.

And never ever forget the Freedom Mantra—**I do my duties free from rewards."**

He said.

Those were his last words. I saw him walking mindfully towards his airplane as we waved good-byes to each other.

I then walked towards my boarding gate, towards my new life, and towards the Freedom Mantra.

Epilogue

This is my story, the seven words—**I do my duties free from rewards**—have transformed my life. Through dedicated practice, I found joy, peace, and of course, freedom.

I Do, is to be focused on doing the work and eliminating laziness.

My Duties, is to understand your duties, that are specific to you, to fulfill the purpose of your life, and to help humanity.

Free from Rewards, is to be free from attachments-repulsions, and to maintain equanimity with the dualities of life (success-failure, good-bad, happiness-sorrow) etc.

The idea is so simple and yet so profound. Freedom Mantra changed my life, and it will change the lives of many restless souls all across humanity.

I found success because I was committed to the Freedom Mantra, and I practiced the two methods taught by the Billionaire Monk, on a daily basis.

Letting Go through Contemplation: (Explained in the chapter, Understanding the Mind). Over the years, I have practiced 'Letting Go through Contemplation' two times daily. This commitment has helped me eliminate the unwanted energy of rewards(attachments-repulsions) from my system. I have learned that the mind needs to be cleaned every day from this unwanted energy. If we don't remove it on a daily basis, we are far far away from freedom.

Remember through Repetition: (Explained in the chapter, Intellect Reprograms the Mind). Over the years, I have repeated the mantra mentally before going to sleep and first thing in the morning hours. Also, I have written the mantra regularly. This has been an essential part of my practice. I had decided to practice the mantra diligently. I understood that the mantra had to resonate with every breath I take.

And through regular practice, I have experienced freedom. This feeling has stayed with me and has deepened with time. Whenever I stumble, from the seat of freedom, all I have to do is practice the mantra.

I have understood that Freedom is a state of Divine wisdom. It's a state of no conflict. It's a state of peace. It's a state of never-ending JOY.

Through the practice of Freedom Mantra, I discovered that excessive thinking stops. The mind understands that there is no need to cling to people, things, or situations. The mind understands that there is no need to worry about rewards. This insight calms the mind.

Through the practice of Freedom Mantra, I discovered that emotional trauma stops. As we eliminate attachments-repulsions and reward-seeking actions, we learn to manage our emotions very quickly. We learn to deal with stressful situations. And we learn to be at peace all the time.

Freedom Mantra is a subtle change. It's a one-degree change, that reprograms the mind, and brings a one-hundred-eighty-degree shift, to our lives. The key to this practice is to practice it every encounter with life.

This is my story. And this is how I found the path to freedom. Even a little practice takes me closer to freedom. Sometimes, I stumble from the anchor of freedom, but then, all I have to do is remember the Freedom Mantra —

I do my duties free from rewards.

About the Author

Kumar Anu is a traveler and storyteller. Through his books, he intends to help humanity find meaning and purpose. The word Moksha (Inner Freedom) became the essence of his life when he started practicing the Freedom Mantra. Freedom Mantra is a simple practice—to do your duties free from rewards.